When I Feel Sad

by Megan B. Mo

Dedication

To my husband; thank you for inspiring me to write this book. I love you, may the pages in these books reach the younger versions of ourselves that needed healing and inspire our future generations to feel their feelings.

Sadness is when you get really big yucky feelings that sometimes you don't know how to explain.

We might not always know how to talk about our big feelings when we are sad.

So let's explore some things that can help us with sad feelings!

When I'm sad, sometimes I cry because it's ok to let the big feelings out, instead of keeping them stuffed in!

When I'm sad, sometimes I take a break in my room, because it's ok to ask for space so I can recharge and feel better

When I'm sad, sometimes I play my games because doing something fun always makes me feel better! Fun things make me smile!

When I'm sad, sometimes I say it out loud because it's ok to say

"I don't feel ok today"

When I'm sad and start to feel upset, I remind myself that it's not nice to be mean to other people or myself, so I ask someone to take me on a walk to cool off!

When I'm sad and start to think everything is hard, I think about things that make me feel happy!
Like:

HA! HA! HA!

a joke, my dog, or my favorite movie!

When I'm sad and think that my feelings are not OK, I remind myself that this feeling will pass and I won't be sad forever!

I will feel better again!

When I'm sad because I miss someone who is far away or not here anymore, I talk about the person I'm missing to others around me. It fills my heart with joy to talk about them!

When I'm sad because I feel left out, I remind myself of the many things I like about myself!

What are three things you like about yourself?

When I'm sad and feel alone, I remind myself that other people get sad too! I'm not the only one!

Next time you get sad, remember that this feeling will pass and pretty soon you'll feel better like I do!

When I'm sad because people are being mean to me, I find a friend who likes me and play games with them!

But when people do or say mean things that hurt my feelings, I have to also remember to tell an adult who can help! Especially if I don't feel safe!

Here are some things that have helped us with our big feelings so you can try them next time too! and remember that if you ever need help with how sad you feel, go talk to an adult!!!

drawing

reading

talking to someone

taking a nap

listening to happy music

watching something funny

crying and
letting it out

thinking
about happy
things

playing with
a pet

taking
space and
saying
"this will
pass!"

spending time
outside

giving someone a hug

playing a game

putting an ice
pack on your head

friends

drinking water

sports

smiling!

Activity time!!

What are some things you can do the next time you feel sad

_____

_____

_____

_____

Who are some people you can talk to about your feelings?

_____

_____

_____

How can you help others when they feel sad?

_____

_____

_____

_____

Made in the USA
Monee, IL
07 October 2024

67278626R00017